To Kevin

With best wishes —

A Glittering Haze

A GLITTERING HAZE

Strategic Advertising in the 1990s

Winston Fletcher

NTC PUBLICATIONS LTD

First published in 1992 by
NTC Publications Limited
Farm Road
Henley-on-Thames
Oxfordshire RG9 1EJ
United Kingdom
Telephone: 0491 574671

A CIP catalogue record for this book is available
from the British Library

ISBN 1-870562-91-7

Typeset in 12/14 pt Garamond
by NTC Publications Ltd
Printed and bound in Great Britain by
Biddles Ltd, Guildford and King's Lynn

For Heavenly People

Contents

I
A glittering haze

Once upon a time hardly a month passed without a new advertising rulebook being published.

'YOU is the most powerful word in the English language ... NEW is the most powerful word in the English language ... Humorous advertising doesn't work because people don't buy from clowns ... no billboard should contain more than 14 words ... every advertisement must contain a Unique Sales Proposition ... coupons should always be in the bottom right-hand corner ... TRUE is the most powerful word in the English language ... but BLUE should never be associated with foods ...'

Greenhorns were required to read, mark, learn and inwardly digest a plethora of such trivial principles as though they were Newtonian laws.

Their authors and inventors propounded them with a huckster's confidence but without very much sound scientific supporting data.

And the advertising world loved them, and clung to them, because they offered certainty in an uncertain world, radar in a glittering haze.

Today almost nobody bothers to search for such quasi-scientific laws, let alone believes them.

This has come about partly because television has become the dominant medium for consumer goods advertising, and it has proved a great deal harder to promulgate plausible rules for TV commercials than for print advertisements.

And anyway television is still a young medium. The first-ever commercial was screened some 50 years ago, whereas print has been around for centuries.

But mostly it is because the vast quantities of research that have been carried out over recent decades have taught the advertising industry that there are no infallible rules.

So despite all the testing and the shmesting, despite all the focus groups and tracking studies, despite all the econometrics and computer analyses, advertising is still largely a hit or miss business. Even today nobody can predict exactly what a campaign will achieve.

Advertising is much more like farming than like physics.

A good farmer will consistently obtain better yields than a bad farmer, but he still can't forecast next year's crop.

'Half my advertising is wasted, but I've no way of knowing which half', the aphorism usually attributed to the first Lord Leverhulme, is still widely, mindlessly, incessantly quoted.

Nowadays, as we'll see, that simple 50 per cent estimate is in some respects wildly optimistic.

Because in the decades since Lord Leverhulme may or may not have coined his clever quip the number of advertisements has grown exponentially, the number of products on the market has grown exponentially, the number of advertising media has grown exponentially, and the uses and functions of advertising have grown more than a little.

But advertising theory has not kept pace with the rapidly increasing diversity of the advertising market place.

Advertising theories have consistently attempted to simplify and impose homogeneity on an increasingly heterogeneous subject, and the attempts were doomed to certain failure.

St Bernards, greyhounds and chihuahuas are all dogs and have many similarities, but you don't need to be a canine connoisseur to spot a fair number of crucial differences between them.

To attempt to squeeze potato crisps, patent medicine and political advertising into the same mould as each other is as futile as it would be to enter a St Bernard in the Greyhound Derby or to send a chihuahua padding through the snows toting a brandy barrel round its tiny neck.

Most of the rulebooks of yesteryear focused on branded consumer goods, though they also derived lessons from direct response advertising.

They assumed that all consumer goods advertisements work in much the same way, and in much the same way as direct response advertising for that matter.

As advertising extended into new fields – politics, social issues, retail, charities – it was assumed that these were simply deviant forms of branded consumer goods, as though greyhounds and chihuahuas were simply deviant forms of St Bernard.

The quest for a formula which will guarantee successful advertising is as futile as the quest for the Holy Grail – not that that will stop people looking: hope springs eternal in the ad-man's breast. It would be wonderful to discover a compass that would guide us unerringly through the glittering haze; but no such compass exists.

Consumers react to advertisements in an infinite variety of ways, and each new advertisement generates subtly different responses from its innumerable predecessors. And the fact that there have been innumerable

predecessors inevitably and in turn influences consumers' responses to each new advertisement.

The average 35-year-old adult will have seen some
150,000 different commercials, most of them many
times. New commercials do not fall on virgin soil –
they are received by seasoned, sceptical advertising-
literate minds. Minds which understand perfectly well
that advertisements convey diverse messages by diverse
means, appealing to diverse emotions in pursuit of
diverse objectives.

Many advertisements persuade people to spend, but
lots persuade them to save; some advertisements tell
people things they don't know, but many tell them
things they know already; some aim to reinforce their
existing loyalties, others aim to make them unfaithful;
many make them laugh but some can bring tears to their
eyes; some may make them question their political
beliefs, others may persuade them to change their jobs,
their houses, their sexual habits or even their very lives.

Having spent some 30 years in the business, I grow
increasingly aware that different products call for
different approaches, that each new campaign is a new
challenge.

You might have thought – I might have hoped –
that by now I would have concluded that all advertising
problems are much of a muchness. Not so.

Naturally this increasing unceasing diversity makes
precise analysis, and precise targeting both especially
difficult and especially vital.

And while it is obviously true that if advertisers did
not want advertising there wouldn't be any, it is equally
true that if consumers did not want advertising there
wouldn't be any: it is mutually beneficial.

Advertising is not something that powerful firms do to powerless (though sometimes stubborn) consumers.

On the contrary, advertising works because consumers want it to work. If consumers didn't want advertising to work, it wouldn't; if they rejected its messages, it would fail.

But they do not reject its messages, because they know advertising benefits them in more ways than they've had frozen dinners.

Advertising introduces people to useful new products and reminds them of old products they had almost forgotten.

Advertising tells people where they can buy goods at low prices and where they can invest their savings at high interest rates.

Advertising informs people where they can go to be entertained and what they can do to alleviate their pains and sufferings.

Advertising lets people know how to use products in ways they had not previously thought of and how to improve themselves in ways they had not previously dreamed of.

Advertising warns people against behaving dangerously and encourages them to behave responsibly.

Advertising adds extra dimensions – of consistency, of glamour, of quality, of reassurance, of value – to the things people buy.

Advertising saves people time by providing them with neatly encapsulated, easily absorbed information.

Advertising provides people with cheap media.

Advertising helps force manufacturers to keep their prices down.

Advertising helps people find new jobs, new homes,

new holidays, new secondhand knick-knacks and even, occasionally, new spouses.

Yet despite all the bounteous benefits it brings, advertising is in the doldrums.

Though advertising people play ostrich with an insouciance which might make even ostriches envious, the evidence is everywhere to be seen.

Having surged forward at a rate of knots for a decade or so, in both Britain and the United States advertising is now drifting backwards.

As a proportion of the Gross National Product, advertising is in decline.

Nor is this a temporary phenomenon: nobody expects the boom times to return in the foreseeable future, in either Britain or America.

Advertisers are increasingly turning to other forms of marketing communication, which are now growing more rapidly than media advertising and which are stealing funds from advertising budgets: database marketing, telemarketing, sponsorship, in-store promotions and the rest.

Even the one activity in which advertising indubitably excels – brand-building – is in decline.

Very few advertisers are building new brands.

'Brand-stretching' – using an existing brand name on new product variants – is the order of the day.

Visit your local supermarket and you will find loads of old brand names on heaps of brand new products.

Why? Because brand stretching is quicker, and safer, and above all cheaper than incurring the advertising costs involved in brand-building.

(Note that product research and development expenditures are still willingly incurred. It is only the advertising expenditures which are baulked at.)

The same is true each time Mega Multinational Inc. snaps up the Mini Marketing Company to acquire its portfolio of brands.

The advertising industry pats itself on the back; but it shouldn't.

'This shows,' the advertising industry proudly proclaims, 'that great companies like Mega Multinational Inc. recognise the real value of famous brands. And Mini Marketing's famous brands were built by brilliant advertising. Which proves conclusively, once and for all, and beyond the shadow of a doubt that advertising is an investment not a cost.'

Well yes and no.

It also proves beyond the shadow of a doubt that Mega Multinational preferred to spend billions of capital – with all the attendant interest costs and cash flow disadvantages – rather than put up the money necessary to build brands of its own.

So instead of spending big bucks on advertising, Mega Multinational Inc has simply swelled the bank balances of Mini Marketing's outgoing shareholders.

That is hardly something for the advertising industry to celebrate.

The industry also likes to congratulate itself that so many of today's leading brands have been around for donkey's years, because this proves their longevity and disproves the discredited theory of brand life-cycles. With careful nurturing and constant advertising, brands, unlike mere mortals, seem able to live forever.

(In his dirgelike tome *Whatever Happened to Madison Avenue?* author Martin Mayer notes that in 16 important US markets the 1923 brand leader was still brand leader more than 60 years later.)

But once again the industry should not be overjoyed by this news.

Old brands can coast. Their advertising-to-sales ratios are much lower than those of infant brands which have to holler to get noticed.

Advertisers' growing lack of confidence in media advertising – well documented in a galaxy of gloomy press articles and research studies[1] – has been reflected in the way they have nibbled away at (and sometimes bitten deep into) the remunerations they pay their agencies.

The labourer, as the old saw goes, is worthy of his hire. If advertisers were as bullish about advertising as they were in days of yore, they would not now be so parsimonious about paying the agencies who create it for them.

Mind you, in many ways the agencies have brought their current difficulties upon themselves.

In reply to their disaffected, faltering clients, agencies have tripped over each other in their rush to claim that creativity is the treatment for all advertising ills.

Great advertising ideas, the agencies chant in unison, still make the cash registers go ting-a-ling and the credit card authorisations go beep-beep-beep.

Marlboro cowboys, Hathaway eyepatches, Benson & Hedges riddles, PG chimps, Hamlet happiness and their heirs and successors will continue to refresh sales

---

[1] To quote just one absolute and unequivocal prognostication, from just one of the world's great advertisers: 'I absolutely and unequivocally do not see a time when advertising budgets will grow like they did in the halcyon days' - Philip Guarascio, General Motors' Executive Director of Advertising Strategies, in the *Newsweek* cover feature *What Happened to Advertising?*, September 1991.

in ways that other marketing communications cannot reach.

None of that can be doubted or disputed.

The power of great advertising, like diamonds, will be forever.

But advertising's current woes do not stem from a lack of creativity. (Though many of the problems have been exacerbated, as we shall see, by misdirected creativity.)

As advertising has burgeoned, and particularly as television has boomed, and as both the market place and the media have fragmented, changes have occurred that have largely passed unnoticed.

Despite the abundant advantages advertising brings them, most advertisements are now of no benefit at all to most people.

I am not in the least bit interested in buying most of the things I see advertised. Indeed I won't buy them. Nor will you.

Nobody is influenced by most of the advertisements they see.

A few individual advertisements benefit each of us, in immeasurable ways, every day of the week; but the great majority of advertisements are irrelevant to us.

In fact things were ever thus: the underlying principle has not changed.

(Maybe that is what drove Lord Leverhulme to reach his sceptical conclusion in the first place.)

But in advertising changes occur at the margin: each year a few more people ignore a few more advertisements, and advertising grows a little less efficient.

Why are more people ignoring more advertisements?

Principally, as we shall see, it is because what the advertisements say is of little interest to them.

Though advertising is still effective, it is not as effective as it might be.

The clock has not quite broken, but it is certainly losing time; it may not yet need a full-scale repair, but it certainly needs an overhaul – starting with the basic mechanism.

II
Faces in the crowd

Each time you walk down a crowded street you see hundreds, maybe thousands of people.

And almost every single one of them passes by unnoticed.

You haven't made a conscious decision to ignore them, it is not as deliberate as that.

Nonetheless you won't remember the great majority of them 30 seconds – let alone 30 minutes or 30 days – later.

It is much the same with advertisements.

A few of the people you pass, a tiny handful, make some impact on you.

You notice them and maybe remember their faces for a few seconds, or even a few hours, or – in exceptional circumstances – for a few days or weeks.

Why do you notice those you notice? Why do you remember those you remember?

Obviously you tend to notice people who are unusual, people who stand out in the crowd (to coin a cliché).

Perhaps they stand out because they are inherently, physically different from other people. They may be strikingly beautiful, or ugly, or even look funny, or charming, or especially aggressive.

Perhaps they stand out simply because they have made themselves seem different. They may be dressed very stylishly, or eccentrically, or be made up garishly; or they may be shouting, or singing, or moving strangely.

And of course they may be both physically different *and* dressed unusually; the one does not preclude the other.

Perhaps, on the other hand, they do not stand out for other people at all. To other people they look quite ordinary, but you notice them because something about them has particular relevance for you, personally.

Perhaps they are wearing something that especially interests you, maybe something you have been searching for or something you particularly like. Maybe you know them already, or they remind you of somebody else; or maybe you seem to keep seeing them, and they are beginning to impinge on your consciousness.

And there is another occasion when you will pick out a face in the crowd: when it is a face you are looking for.

When you are searching for someone in a throng it often seems as though you can see everyone else but them. In reality your eyes are rapidly skimming across dozens and dozens of faces, without taking them in, until finally they alight on the correct one – if it is there to be found.

These interactions and relationships are exactly replicated in people's reactions to advertisements. And they reveal that there are four, and only four, basic reasons why people notice and remember advertisements.

First because the product is inherently different; second, because the advertisement itself is unusual; third, because the advertisement has some particular, personal relevance to them (they may even have been searching for it); fourth, because it is an advertisement they seem to keep seeing.

As with faces in the crowd, these are not mutually exclusive. Advertising works best, is most noticeable and memorable, when all four of these factors are at work simultaneously – when it is an unusual advertisement, which you seem to keep seeing, for a product that is different and has relevance for your personally.

But many advertisers, and many agencies, concentrate on one or two of the four factors. And their advertising works, to some extent. Almost all advertising works, to some extent.

Every day most people are exposed to hundreds, maybe thousands of advertisements but almost all of them pass unnoticed.

Media Register – the country's leading advertising expenditure analysts – pick up about 850,000 display advertisements in newspapers and magazines each year. That's about 2,350 per day. And Media Register only scrutinise 500 of the 9,000 or so publications currently available.

To the press and magazines must be added posters and television spots, radio commercials and direct mail shots, movie trailers and matchbox covers, perimeter placards and propagandist badges, seaside skywriters and sandwich-board men ...

How many of these advertisements does the average person see in a day? Nobody knows. Specious surveys have sought to establish an exact figure but you only need to think about it for a second to realise that the question is all but meaningless.

(How many people do you see in a day? Should you count all the people on the buses, in the shops, on the streets? Should you count all the people at the extreme edge of your vision, or only those you really look at?)

It is the same with advertisements. Should you count all the small ads, as you turn over the pages of your morning newspaper, should you add all the billboards on the distant horizon?

No? But maybe you should, because if they contain something that really interests you they will probably catch your eye.

How many advertisements does the average person see in a day? An awful lot.

How many register? A tiny few.

Why?

Because of the extraordinary mechanism by which our eyes, in concert with our brains, pick out and notice particular items from the morass of visual data which assails them at every waking moment: the mechanism of *selective perception*.

Selective perception is the mechanism underlying the four factors which will make some advertisements noticeable and memorable while most are neither.

It seems to be a protective mechanism which *Homo sapiens* has developed because the brain could never cope with all the sense data – not to mention all the advertising – which bombards it from morning till night.

(Perhaps, in some remote pre-historic era, a species existed which tried to process and remember every single titbit it saw and heard and smelt and tasted. No wonder that species failed to survive: it must have gone stark raving barmy.)

Selective perception is still hardly understood by psychologists[2], but is of immense importance in advertising.

[2] The intractible difficulty involved in the experimental investigation of selective perception is that human beings can only report on those perceptions they know they have had, and are aware of, not on those perceptions which they do not know they have had, and so are unaware of. That may sound obvious to you, but it gives psychologists awful headaches.

Selective perception is simultaneously advertising's best friend and worst enemy.

It is the reason why we often notice advertisements, no matter how small, which are carrying messages of personal relevance to us.

But it is also the barrier that advertisements must constantly strive to overcome in order to communicate their messages to people who have not made a conscious decision to ignore them – it is not as deliberate as that – but whose minds are protecting themselves against information overload.

In days gone by, long ago, people did not meet that many people, so it probably was not all that difficult to get to know a high proportion of them. And in days gone by, long ago, there were fewer products available, and far, far fewer advertisements, so it probably was not that difficult to get to know a high proportion of them.

Nowadays we are inundated with products, with advertisements, (and with people). We can probably cope with more than our forefathers could – though even that is unproven – but the *percentage* of the total is shrinking. That cannot be avoided.

Indeed the evidence suggests that the percentage is shrinking pretty damn quick. The US market research company Video Storyboard Tests claims that in 1986 64 per cent of Americans could name a TV commercial they had seen in the previous four weeks; just five years later, in 1990, the figure had shrunk to 48 per cent.

Living in today's crowded world of advertising is a little like visiting China.

In China you are rapidly overwhelmed by the astronomical numbers of people. It is utterly impossible to encompass them all. So in practice you respond only to those who somehow or other get through to you – those who leap the hurdle of your selective perception[3].

To overcome the barrier of selective perception most advertisements need to intrude; they need to squeeze their messages into people's already junk-laden minds. In current advertising jargon they need to have impact, to build awareness.

Which naturally leads us to investigate the nature of intrusion.

---

[3] It must certainly be the case that some people are much better than others at remembering advertisements – just as some people are much better than others at remembering faces. Whether some people are more likely than others to *respond* to advertisements is more doubtful. In any event, to the best of my knowledge, nowhere in the world has either subject ever been investigated. Both would be worthy of study.

III

Knocking on the mind's door

Before analysing the nature of intrusion we will need to sketch in an impressionist picture of the crowded world of advertising as seen from the consumers' vantage point.

Let's start by remembering (because it is usually forgotten) that a massive amount of advertising is not intrusive at all. And in many respects the unintrusive advertising is much more important than the intrusive advertising.

About a quarter of all the money spent on advertising goes on classifieds. Every day hundreds of thousands, maybe millions of classified advertisements appear. Once again nobody knows the exact number – but there must be at least a hundred times more, and quite possibly a thousand times more, classified than display ads. There cannot be a single literate adult who has not at some time responded to a classified advertisement, and indeed very few who have not placed one for themselves.

(That is one reason why the mythical Mr and Mrs Average understand advertising far better than they are often given credit for. Everyone has produced the occasional Darts Club Dinner and Dance poster, or sold a second-hand stuffed camel in their local free-sheet.)

Patently, classified advertisements are not intrusive: the reader seeks them out.

The classified sections include advertisements for jobs, homes, holidays, entertainments, births, marriages, deaths (and Valentines). Of these, job advertising is much the largest sector, by value, accounting for about one-third of the total, and thus about 10 per cent of all advertising.

And there are few things more important to most of us than our jobs, our homes, our holidays and our entertainments – not to mention our births, marriages, deaths (and Valentines).

However important we judge our choice of deodorant or detergent to be, it hardly compares with our choice of a new job or a new house.

Even the large display advertisements for houses in magazines like *Country Life* are not truly intrusive: they are all bunched together so people will know where to find them.

Indeed I have often wondered why television and radio stations don't carry similar 'classified' sections, at well-publicised times on specific days, when all job ads, or house ads, or personal ads could be bundled together and those who are interested could watch out for them. But then, to me the ways of the media owners have always been a riddle wrapped in an enigma.

Nor are classifieds the only advertisements people seek out.

Much retail price-and-line advertising is built upon the premise that lots of people will be looking for particular items, and searching for the lowest prices. Whether it be butter or bitter, a 3-piece suite or a Panasonic VCR, those who scan retail advertisements generally have a fair idea of what they are looking for, in advance.

On the other hand, they may not know precisely which product they want: they may just be looking for a bargain or two.

Either way it is the shopper who does most of the

work, rather than the advertisement.

Beyond communicating quickly that it contains loads of bargains, the advertisement hardly needs to intrude; the shopper is a willing accomplice. Unfortunately not one advertising person in a hundred seems to understand this.

And a further group of advertisements which people look out for, when they are relevant to them, are financial offers.

If you happen to have some cash which you are contemplating investing – a windfall perhaps, or hard-won savings – then you will scour the Personal Finance pages for the best offer on offer. If you are desperate for a mortgage or other kind of loan, you will do the same.

Such advertisements do not need to intrude.

They simply need to flag those who are looking for them. But if you are not particularly thinking of a new mortgage, or a loan, the advertisement will need to tap you on the shoulder and bring itself to your attention. It will need to make you think about all the wonderful things you could do if you borrowed some more dosh.

So some financial advertisements can be small and undemonstrative, while others have to be bigger and noisier. It depends on the objective, and on the target market.

Yet another group of advertisements which hardly intrude are those in hobby publications. Advertisements for photographic equipment in *Amateur Photographer*, fishing tackle in *Angling Times*, D-I-Y materials in *Practical Householder* and the like.

Everybody agrees – even the disgruntled editors – that people buy such publications as much for the advertisements as for the editorial.

The products advertised reflect the hobbyists' interests, their commitment to their leisure and pleasure. So the advertisements are important to them.

As are many industrial, business-to-business advertisements in trade and technical publications. These often provide news and information which industrial purchasers are looking for and find useful.

That is the principle reason why industrial advertising was always permissible in the Communist bloc countries; it was deemed to be useful rather than persuasive (as if such simple dividing lines could be drawn!).

If you add together all classified advertising, including recruitment, some of the retail advertising, some of the financial advertising, hobby advertising, and some business-to-business advertising, then it can be no exaggeration to say that in total 40-50 per cent of all advertising is non-intrusive. They are all advertisements which people patently want: people look for them of their own volition.

And you might tack on another group of small ads, classic patent medicine advertisements.

You know the type. They flag the sufferer with such succulent headlines as 'Acne?' or 'Piles?' or 'Embarrassing Irritation?'. They are perfect examples of selective perception at work.

These small medicine advertisements spotlight the borderline between intrusion and self-interest. They depend upon readers' consciousness of their ailments. To some extent the readers are sub-consciously on the look-out for a remedy. But the advertisements also need to penetrate the reader's mind, because the reader may not be consciously searching for a remedy at that precise moment.

At the time the individuals are suffering, treating the ailment may seem quite as important to them as finding a new job or house. That is why small medicine advertisements are not unlike classifieds: the advertiser can rely on the reader's selective perception doing much of the work.

The less work the reader is willing to do, the more intrusive the advertising must be.

Many things that are advertised are not of immense importance to us, and unless they are drawn to our attention we won't bother to watch out for them. In fact we don't bother to think much about them at all.

As Jean-Michel Agostini and Michael Brulé[4] have shown – and as common-sense happily confirms – the intensity of people's interest in different product categories (and hence in the advertising for different product categories) varies vastly, from utter indifference to manic obsession.

Not many people would peruse the classifieds for a toothpaste advertisement in the way they will do for a holiday or a home. Houses and holidays are worthy of considerable attention and effort; nowadays toiletries, by and large, are not – though in days gone by toiletries were probably pretty engrossing too.

(My agency recently carried out research on some immensely witty but immensely wordy deodorant advertisements. Despite the fact that they regularly use the product, the housewives who were shown the campaign were not amused. 'Who could expect us to read so much stuff about a mere deodorant?' they asked

---

[4] All references are detailed in the Bibliography.

irritably, 'it's not worth the trouble. It's quicker to go buy it and find out for yourself.')

On the face of it intrusion occurs at the behest of the advertiser, and provides little benefit to the consumer. Surely if the consumers really want something they should be willing to go searching for it?

Why can't all advertisements be classifieds, activated by people who are genuinely interested in them, rather than big jobs produced by people who want to foist their messages onto others – and onto others who apparently don't want to receive them?

That is how print advertising began.

Once, in the 1960s, I met the great Lord Chief Justice Lord Goddard and he asked what I did for a living. 'Advertising,' I replied nervously.

'Advertising! Advertising!' he boomed. 'You mean the front page of *The Times* and that sort of thing?'

The good Lord, well into his eighties, was recalling an era already then past, when the entire front pages of quality newspapers were crowded with little classifieds, and people presumably had both the time and the inclination to pore over them – an era when even toiletries, perhaps, were well worth reading about.

Nowadays there is too little time, and there are too many products. People frequently do not know whether or not they are interested in a particular product, or service, or warning, or whatever, until an advertisement knocks on their mind's door and tells them about it; and often they need to be told again and again before they take any notice.

This is a widely misunderstood phenomenon.

Advertising's antagonists believe it proves advertisements make people buy things they don't really want.

The reality is far simpler.

If you drive along the M40 motorway you will see a sign, north of Oxford, saying 'Historic Warwick'.

It is not really a directional road sign: you can tell that because it is brown, not blue, and because it rhymes so nicely.

It is a discreet advertisement.

Although it is restrained and simple the sign, like all road signs, is visual clutter; it sullies England's green and pleasant land; it is deliberately placed in a position where you can hardly avoid noticing it; it is intrusive[5].

Let us presume that before spotting it you had not the least intention of visiting Historic Warwick.

The sign makes you think of doing something you were not previously going to do.

Something you may well enjoy.

Just as commercials make you think of doing things – buying things, or using things – you were not previously going to do.

Things you may well enjoy. That's hardly devious unless you start from the assumption that human beings know exactly what they want, at all times, and never need nudging. And that is patent nonsense.

The intellectuals and academics who criticise advertising doubtless always know precisely how they want to spend their time and what they wish to spend their money on. The rest of us are more malleable. And in my view that's no disadvantage.

For the Historic Warwick sign to get its simple

---

[5] Ogden Nash versified:
'I think that I shall never see
A billboard lovely as a tree
Indeed, unless the billboards fall
I'll never see a tree at all'.

message across it was necessary for it to intrude. The sign had to jut itself into the passing motorist's mind.

But the power of intrusion should not be exaggerated.

The sign could not force you to visit Historic Warwick. It could not pick you up by the scruff of the neck, twist your arm behind your back or put a pistol to your head. It does not even employ deep, psychological witchcraft to achieve its persuasive aims.

Similarly advertisements – real advertisements – cannot force people to do things they do not want to do.

Nor do the rules allow advertisements to frighten people into doing things they do not want to do, except in cases where appeals to fear can clearly be justified – like road safety, or AIDS.

The Historic Warwick sign, like all real advertisements, is far more likely to work if it falls on fertile ground. It is far more likely to work if it is seen by ye olde tea shoppe freaks, members of the National Trust, folk who rush out every spring to buy their annual copy of *Historic Houses, Castles and Gardens Open to the Public* hot off the press.

Indeed they will probably welcome the intrusion.

It will certainly intrude on their consciousness far more easily than it will penetrate the consciousness of those passing drivers to whom visiting old castles would be about as much fun as watching lavatory cleanser commercials for hours on end without a break.

For they will not welcome the intrusion; they may even wonder why Historic Warwick has been permitted to litter the countryside with its publicity.

In other words, the intrusion will be welcomed by some and disliked by others: that is a general truth

about all advertising. And it has had profound consequences on the way advertising, particularly television
advertising, has developed over recent years.

Back on the M40, you've seen the discreet sign, but
you can't nip off for a visit today because you are
terribly late for a meeting.

So you forget about it.

At least you think you have forgotten.

But in subsequent months you occasionally pass the
sign again. It keeps right on intruding.

And eventually you give in.

To open the mind's door it is often necessary to keep
on knocking.

But the castle haters will never give in; and to them
the intrusive road sign could easily become increasingly
irritating – like a commercial for a product you do not
like.

For the purpose of this little scenario you were in the
target market. Indeed you were a keen member of the
target market, personally interested in mediaeval
moated castles and suchlike. That is why you were
willing to respond to a bland sign lacking any persuasive copy. Others would take more convincing.

If the wily wizards in Historic Warwick's marketing
department had had a free hand with the design of the
sign it would almost certainly be possible to increase
the number of visitors. A pretty picture of the castle
turrets and some witty words about the dungeons
would doubtless work wonders.

Yet still only a small proportion of those who saw
the sign would nip off the motorway across the draw-
bridge and past the castle's portcullis.

In this respect the Historic Warwick sign works just

like the advertising for all other famous brands – if it isn't too irreverent to call Historic Warwick a brand like all the rest.

(Not a fast-moving packaged good, admittedly; more of a consumer durable.)

IV
Maybe 96 per cent is wasted

One of the maddeningly confusing things about advertising is that it uses mass media to communicate with quite small audiences.

The Historic Warwick road sign is a mass medium – well it is seen by masses of motorists – but at best it will persuade only tens of thousands each year to visit the town.

It is exactly the same with television, newspapers and magazines, radio and cinema – and even sandwich-board men for that matter – but the strands are more difficult to disentangle.

Even major campaigns are really targeted at quite small minorities. Or anyway, they should be.

The fact that they have not been is one of the principle ways in which advertising has gone astray.

If you visit a supermarket you may leave with 30, 40 or perhaps even 50 items listed on your check-out bill. The average number of items of all kinds purchased per visit is currently about 20.

Many of these – fruit, vegetables, fresh meat, delicatessen and so on – will not be advertised brands; some of the others will be multiple purchases of the same brand.

At a maximum (and if you have a gargantuan and incredibly picky family!) you will have bought a couple of dozen advertised brands – out of the 15,000 lines on sale in the store. Over the course of a year your brand choices will swing about a bit, but you are exceedingly unlikely to buy more than a few hundred different brands annually.

If you are a husband, however, you may never visit

a supermarket at all; men are only responsible for about one-third of supermarket purchases. On the other hand, you probably visit the pub from time to time, as 65 per cent of men go to a pub once a month or more.

There, during the course of a year, you may imbibe a dozen or so different brands of booze, but probably far fewer.

If you are in charge of the family's finances you may make a small number of investment decisions during the year; it is most unlikely that you will change your bank.

Consumer durables? Maybe a dozen a year, if you're a consumer durables freak.

Cars? In Britain your car may well be supplied by your employers. If it isn't you only buy one every three years.

And though it may seem otherwise when you study your wardrobe and your bank balance, you do not buy that many clothes either; and most of them will not be advertised brands, because there is not that much advertising of clothes.

Even when you throw in confectionery, medicines, hardware, all the services you can think of and the kitchen sink (a new one every decade or so) it is virtually certain that you do not buy more than 400 different brands in a year.

One day, in the not-too-distant future, it will be possible to get the precise figure – if you are Mr and Mrs Average – from a computer.

But for the moment an estimate will do, and 400 is unquestionably the maximum.

Here's another rough-and-ready way to get at the same figure.

If you have about 25 minutes to spare, and if you wouldn't find it too tedious, wander around your house and count all the advertised brands.

Remember to count all the consumer durables, and – if you are horticulturally inclined – to look in the garden shed.

You will need to make some arbitrary decisions, particularly about retailers' own brands, and about different varieties of the same brand: but in this instance precise exactitude is not called for, a few more or a few less won't make much difference.

I have just done it, and I counted 143 advertised brands.

(I excluded my books, because they hardly constitute advertised brands, and anyway many of them are old advertising books which contradict everything I am saying!)

I don't wish to sound boastful, but the likelihood is that I probably own as many brands, of whatever, as Mr and Mrs Average.

And obviously, once again, my own and my family's brand choices change during the course of each year; and we buy a few branded services – financial, holidays, travel and the like – which can't be kept in the larder.

But on the basis of this extremely scientific piece of research, a purchase level of 400 brands a year again looks like the absolute maximum.

Compare that with the 32,500 branded goods and services that, according to Media Register, are currently advertised.

Let us even ignore the 23,000 or so which spend less than £50,000 a year, and concentrate on the 9,500 that

Media Register individually list and analyse.

Mr and Mrs Average have bought 400 out of the 9,500 brands being advertised to them. Not every one of those brands is aimed at them, obviously; but the majority of them are.

Remember we are being generous about that 400 figure. And remember, too, that by no means all of those 400 brands will have been bought because of their advertising. Some will have been bought because of word-of-mouth recommendation, others because the packaging looked appealing, still others on whim.

Even without a PhD in mathematics it is easy to see that Mr and Mrs Average have been influenced, *at the very maximum*, by only 400 out of 9,500 brand campaigns: that's 4 per cent.

So you could say at least 96 per cent of all advertising is wasted, but nobody knows which 96 per cent.

And on the classified advertising side you would need a powerful electron microscope to identify the minute proportion of small ads to which people respond.

Does that mean all those millions and millions of advertisements which have failed to persuade them were just money down the drain?

Yes and no.

Waste is inherent in the use of media for advertising.

The notion that every reader of a publication, or every viewer of a commercial break, might immediately rush out and buy all the products advertised is about as silly as the notion propounded by the wonderfully dotty Canadian Professor Wilson Bryan Key, in his wonderfully dotty book *Subliminal Seduction*. Professor Key is convinced that SEX is subconsciously embedded in all advertising.

('Twenty-six advertisements in a recent issue of *Life* magazine had the word *come* in the advertising copy' is probably my favourite-ever quotation. 'Subliminal SEX is today an integral part of modern American advertising... Every major advertising agency has at least one embedding technician in its art department' runs it a close second.)[6]

Professor Key is merely one of a multitude of commentators and theorists who, perplexed by the apparent power of advertising, have sought to uncover its secret magic ingredient, as though it were a detergent.

'All advertising must contain A UNIQUE SELLING PROPOSITION ... powerful ADDED VALUE', they trill. (Or in Professor Key's case, SEX.)

But advertising doesn't have a single magic ingredient, because it isn't a single homogeneous entity. The power of advertising is real, but it is limited.

Back to the grindstone. (Sorry, Professor.)

As we have already noted, people register only a tiny number of the advertisements they see.

They ignore the rest, the great swirling majority, so waste cannot be avoided.

That does not mean advertising isn't cost-effective. Millions and millions of advertisements, every day and throughout the course of history, have repeatedly proved it is.

Advertising has to communicate with large numbers of people in order to reach the relevant minority – because the advertiser cannot know, in advance, exactly

---

[6] When Professor Key raised his dark obsessions with consumerist officials in Washington they spurned him. 'Never known an advertising man smart enough', one of them said sapiently.

which individuals will respond to his blandishments.

Indeed the single, simple reason why media advertising works is that – despite its much-publicised expense – it is still an astonishingly cheap means of mass communication.

A national peak-time 30-second commercial will reach 1,000 people for about £4. To reach 1,000 people by direct mail, in contrast, will cost more than £200.

For £200 the television advertiser will net 50,000 people, a fair number of whom will be customers and potential customers.

At £4 per 1,000 advertising can encompass waste and still deliver results economically, cost-effectively.

Nonetheless all waste is gruesome.

With smart targeting the advertiser can minimise waste by increasing the *percentage* of readers or viewers who will respond; but he can never know *precisely* who will respond.

But then not even the most accurate and finely tuned direct mail shot can ever achieve 100 per cent response.

This is one of the fundamental differences between the use of media and face-to-face selling. It is possible, just, to envisage a salesman scoring with every prospect he speaks to. The same could never happen when media are used.

Indeed if the advertiser knew exactly which people were going to respond there would be no point in using media at all. The advertiser could communicate with them directly.

This is as true of Birth, Marriage, and Death notices as it is of Coca-Cola commercials.

(The only exception I can think of is Valentine advertisements. But Valentine advertisements are really a deliberate misuse of advertising, employed to demonstrate love and devotion through conspicuous waste.)

The art of the buyer of advertising media is to reach the maximum number of customers likely to respond, at the minimum possible cost.

But the phrase 'likely to respond' begs a question, because the media choice can itself increase or decrease people's likelihood to respond.

In this context, the media choice does not only mean television versus press versus radio versus posters versus... It also means whether the advertisement is big or small, long or short, in colour or black/white, where it appears in the publication or when it appears on air, and how often, over what duration of time, and in which months and maybe on what days.

In other words all the variables and factors involved in the selection of advertising media.

Much to everyone's chagrin there is no general, universal answer to the question 'What is the ideal media schedule?'

Horses for courses is the name of the game.

And as with horses, even if the course is right the steed won't perform well if the jockey, the weather or its digestion are not on song.

There are no certainties in racing or in advertising.

But here are some worthwhile tips.

Because the public is increasingly knowledgeable about advertising – research shows that toddlers can now differentiate the commercials from the programmes by the age of three – they know it costs a packet.

So they know big advertisements are more prestigious than small advertisements, and more important.

And they know that national media are more prestigious than local media, and more important.

(That is one reason why local media almost never pull coupon enquiries as effectively as national media.)

They know, or think they know, that television is the most expensive and most important advertising medium, and they tend to believe, of every advertisement they can remember, that they probably saw it on television first. (So there is little point in asking them where they saw such and such an advertisement: they're almost bound to say on television.)

In print media bigger advertisements are more intrusive than smaller advertisements, and so they are seen by more people.

The correlation is not perfect. Whole pages are not seen by quite twice as many people as half-pages, nor are half-pages seen by quite twice as many as quarter-pages, etc. etc.

Nonetheless, as a useful generalisation, on average you get what you pay for in terms of number of readers per column centimetre.

If you think you are economising by buying smaller advertisements, remember all it means is that fewer people will see them.

And the same applies to poster sites.

Unless, that is, you can employ selective perception to ensure that although fewer see them, those who do so are the ones especially interested in what the advertisement is saying.

All this has been confirmed by innumerable Reading and Noting studies.

The fact that big 'uns use more paper and ink, and so are more expensive to produce, would be of little consequence if advertisers had not discovered over the years that the extra cost is often worth it.

The same principle does not apply to the broadcast media.

Longer commercials are not seen by more people than shorter commercials in the same break; nor do they cost any more to transmit.

However it is widely believed that long commercials are remembered by more people than shorter commercials, and that justifies their extra cost.

This may well be true – it seems logical – though I have never seen evidence to prove it.

It is certainly true that broadcast advertisements rely on memory to far greater degree than print advertisements.

Commercials are fleeting, and terribly hard to pore over. It's not that easy to tear them out and take them down to the shops, either.

This is why most people in advertising now believe that advertisements should promise one thing and one thing only. They automatically think of television as the archetypical form of advertising. And television depends upon memory, and because people's memories are already overcrowded simple messages are best.

This is the basis of the famous Unique Selling Proposition theory of advertising which was invented and developed by the Ted Bates agency in the early, pioneering days of television.

The Unique Selling Proposition theory, which has influenced almost all advertising for the last 30 years, is widely misinterpreted.

It is widely thought to mean that advertisements can only promise 'one thing' about a product or service.

Whereas perhaps the single most famous example of

USP advertising is a *double* promise: M & M's famous slogan 'Melts in the mouth, not in the hand'.

And Fairy's 'Hands that do dishes can feel soft as your face' is a double promise too.

As is Sainsbury's 'Where good food costs less'.

Even 'Refreshes the parts other beers cannot reach' is a double promise (refreshment and strength).

While Mars Bars' claim that they help you 'work, rest and play' is arguably a *triple* promise.

As was Hoover's historic 'It beats as it sweeps as it cleans'.

The struggle to encapsulate every product's advantages in a single benefit often castrates the message – and castrates the effectiveness of the advertising.

If a brand has hydra-headed advantages then the creative task is to find a nimble way to say so.

But this must not be an excuse for sloppy thinking. A double promise is not the same as a blurred promise.

Direct response advertisers know they can pack piles of promises and products into the same print advertisement.

And retailers have come to the same conclusion.

But that is because those are the type of advertisements which people study and re-study and even tear out.

In the case of direct response the purchase is made *while* the advertisement is being read: the order form is an intrinsic part of the ad. Memory is irrelevant.

Television could hardly work more differently.

That is why television, even with Freefone numbers, is rarely an effective direct response medium – particularly in peak-time, when costs are high.

And it is why the theories derived from direct response advertising, the results of which can be analysed with great precision, rarely apply to television – or to shop-bought goods generally.

Most advertising depends upon memory; direct response advertising does not. That is about as fundamental a difference as can be.

Posters are like television: the messages must be brief, and must be remembered. Tesco tends to frown on customers who arrive carrying 48-sheet billboards. Classifieds, in contrast, are almost all direct response advertisements.

Broadcast advertising still works in the way the first recorded town criers' advertising worked.

In ancient Greece the town criers, whose principle job was the proclamation of new laws, soon learned that they could earn themselves a few extra drachmas by interspersing their official announcements with commercials.

And Aesclyptoe, an early Athenian Max Factor, promoted his lotions and potions with a commercial which might have sprung yesterday from a highly-paid copywriter's pen:

'For eyes that are shining, for cheeks like the dawn,
For beauty that lasts after girlhood has gone,
For prices in reason, the women who know
Will buy their cosmetics from Aesclyptoe'.

The town crier interrupted his own programmes to broadcast Aesclyptoe's commercial, just as Heineken and the Halifax interrupt the 10 o'clock news.

Through their open windows the Athenian damsels and their menfolk heard it and a few of them – presumably not the men – remembered it when they next visited the Parthenon Boots.

Those who were most likely to remember and so to respond were those who thought they would get some benefit from Aesclyptoe's rejuvenating wares: to them it was a welcome interruption.

To the rest it was doubtless a mild irritation.

And unless Aesclyptoe was the only cosmetician in town most of his audience – perhaps as many as 96 per cent – were unlikely to buy his goods.

Still, netting 4 per cent of the population with a single campaign wouldn't be bad, even in ancient Athens.

In modern Britain that would total about two million customers.

Most advertisements would be doing exceptionally, extraordinarily well if they achieved even half that – a million new customers, or just two per cent of the population.

V

Smart targeting

As today's Western economies grow increasingly diverse and increasingly fragmented by the nanosecond – with brand monopolies ceasing to exist for both competitive and legislative reasons – precise targeting is inevitably becoming the essence of successful marketing.

Market segmentation (née horses for courses) is the name of the game.

Yet defining the target market is one of the most underrated and most difficult parts of the advertising process.[7]

A recent study among 800 British advertisers showed that some 35 per cent of them felt they unnecessarily waste money as a result of poor targeting.

I will bet my personal Panasonic pocket calculator to half-a-dozen focus group discussions that that figure is a massive under-estimate. I will bet that at least 96 per cent of them unnecessarily waste money as a result of poor targeting. (Though I'll admit I don't know *which* 96 per cent!)

Target markets are far tinier than is commonly supposed; and as a result they can usually be defined far

---

[7] I am concentrating here on existing brands. Launching new brands (of which, as we have seen, there is something of a dearth) is a wholly different ballgame. New brands generally need to cast their net as widely as possible as rapidly as possible, to introduce themselves quickly to those who will become their core users. And the same is true, incidentally, of the re-launch of failing brands – though this is an immensely complex subject, and the right targeting strategy to adopt will depend upon a detailed analysis of why the brand is failing and an equally detailed analysis of exactly how and why the brand is to be rejuvenated. I might add, in passing, that in my own experience few seriously failing brands have ever been successfully re-launched. It is a phenomenon much talked about but rarely achieved.

more precisely than is commonly supposed.

Long, long ago, when production lines and economies of scale were a trifle primitive everyone doubtless wore similar loincloths and wielded similar flintstones. A chap's furry wardrobe might be a guide to his wealth, but not to his personality.

In the early days of communism, and during Mao's cultural revolution standardisation ruled – both because it is cheaper for everyone to dress the same, and because it irons out personal idiosyncrasies.

Uniform, after all, means uniform.

Affluence means diversity.

And this is increasingly reflected in brand choice.

Although the average person probably buys fewer than 400 brands a year, we can be confident that half-a-century ago the figure would have been a fifth or maybe only a tenth of that number. Compared with the past, 400 represents sumptuous variety.

And the consequence of this variety is that individual branded products are not bought by vast numbers of people; the huge range of choices means that – on average – fewer people buy each of them.

In these days of mass manufacture there are almost no mass brands.

The days of Henry Ford's famous dictum, 'You can have any colour you like as long as it's black' are long since past.

No branded products are bought regularly by a majority – meaning literally more than 50 per cent – of the adult population, and only a handful are bought by as many as one-third. (Remember that the population includes men as well as women, and that not all women are housewives.)

To convince yourself of the validity of this vital marketing truth, skip through the tables in the Target Group Index – the most accurate and authoritative data source available – and see how many people 'ever buy' even the most major brands.

Here are the approximate percentages for Britain's six top-selling groceries:

	Approximate percentage of adults who 'ever buy' (NB people, not homes)
Ariel	15%
Persil	15%
Nescafé	20%
Whiskas	10%
Andrex	30%
Coca-Cola	35%

The figures are approximate because (a) they vary slightly over time, and (b) some brands come in different varieties – thus emphasising, incidentally, both the diversity of the marketplace and the ubiquity of 'brand-stretching'.

If those are the country's half-a-dozen grocery brand leaders, imagine how few people ever buy the great majority of the 9,500 or so branded goods and services advertised each year and listed by Media Register.

(And don't forget poor old 23,000 itsy-bitsy brands which advertise but are not even deemed worthy of individual recognition by Media Register.)

As Professor Andrew Ehrenberg first demonstrated in his classic study *Repeat-Buying*, today's great brands tend to have a high frequency of purchase rather than a high penetration of usage.

As he also showed, 80 per cent of the sales of any grocery brand are generally accounted for by heavy buyers – those who buy six times a year or more.

Heavy buyers are normally only 25-30 per cent of 'ever buyers'. So that in terms of the total population, the heavy buyers are minorities of minorities.

If those are the figures for grocery brands, the figures for other product fields are even weenier.

With the exception of jug kettles, there is not a single consumer durable bought by as many as five per cent of adults in an average year; jug kettles are bought by six per cent

Financial 'brands' – banks, insurance companies, building societies and the rest – gain, at best, hundreds of thousands of customers each year; four hundred thousand customers is less than one per cent of all adults.

And successful though they were, even the massive privatisation campaigns only sold shares to quite small proportions of the population.

Similarly political campaigns, which are ostensibly aimed at the entire electorate, really influence only the potential floating voters – a fraction of all voters (who anyway comprise only about 70 per cent of the population).

While most other forms of advertising – corporate campaigns, recruitment and the like – are aimed at percentages that are microscopic.

As are the anti-AIDS and drunken driving drives – but that is not to say they aren't worthwhile.

Nor, at the other end of the scale, are the supermarkets

quite so universally used as might be imagined. TGI shows that about 13 million adults shop at Sainsbury's (30 per cent of the population), while 12 million or so shop at Tesco, and at Marks and Spencer.

Now turn these figures upside-down. They prove that even the most hugely popular branded products are never bought by most people.

While for the vast majority of brands the vast majority of people never buy them at all.

Yet there are few brands, few products, few services which would not relish – indeed would not be blissfully happy – if they achieved a 50 per cent sales increase in one year.

For any major, well-established brand, real growth of 10-15 per cent would be more than warmly welcomed.

How many 'new customers' would be required to provide such gains? Two per cent or three per cent of the population *at most*. Often less than one per cent of all adults.

One per cent of adults spending, say, £12 on a brand in a year would deliver an extra £5,000,000 sales – not to be sniffed at even by the Ariels, Persils and Nescafés of the world, let alone by their myriads of smaller competitors and cousins.

Who are these small groups of people?

This, obviously, is the essence of targeting.

In advance, it is impossible to know who they are; but it is possible to know a fair bit about them.

Just as, dear reader, I have not the vaguest idea who you are; but I probably know a fair bit about you.

Not the most intimate details of your sex life or anything of that ilk (despite Professor Key's fantasies).

But if you are reading this it is almost certain that you are a member of the managerial class, involved directly or indirectly in advertising and marketing, that you have a company car, and a mortgage, and all the appurtenances that accompany your status and role in life.

You probably enjoyed (enjoyed?) some higher education, you read the posh Sunday papers, you holiday abroad, you do not watch much television, you eat out quite frequently, and you drink a great deal more than the national average consumption of wine.

(The average Brit drinks less than three glasses of wine a week – so I can be reasonably confident I got that guess right, at least).

Above all, and most importantly, if you are reading this it is as sure as God made little hypotheses that you have read other articles and books about advertising in the past. And quite a few of them, at that.

It is just possible that this is the first time you have read anything even remotely serious about advertising, that this is – so to speak – a virginal experience; but it is most unlikely.

The relevant and significant thing about this conclusion is that not very many of the population bother to read vaguely serious books and articles about advertising: hundreds of thousands at the most.

Yet I was able to guess that you belonged to that eccentric minority.

And without having met you! And without even consulting my personal pocket crystal ball!

Isn't that a miracle?

No.

It is crashingly obvious.

Just as it is crashingly obvious that the people who have given to charities in the past will be those most likely to give to charities in the future; that those who have bought by mail in the past will be those most likely to buy by mail in the future; that those who watched lots of television last year are those most likely to watch lots of television next year. And so on.

And what is more relevant and significant still, in terms of targeting, is that among those people who have *not* given to charities in the past, or who have *not* bought by mail, or who did *not* watch much television, those most likely to be converted will be similar to those who already do whatever it is.

Just as it was easy for me to postulate that most of the people reading this book would share many similar characteristics of ownership and lifestyle.

And all of this applies equally to branded goods and services.

People who choose the same brand, or the same shop, or the same service are to some degree like each other – and to that degree share some similarity of taste or need.

To the degree, at least, that out of the plethora of products and services available, they choose the same ones.

We are all half-conscious this is the case, all the time.

We talk about Sainsbury shoppers and have a loose image of them being rather like each other – just as BMW drivers are all the same (well, more or less), and men who buy their suits at Marks and Spencer are making a bit of a statement about themselves, as are people who drink Martini or Mateus Rosé or serve OK Sauce or Birds Eye Fish Fingers or drive Volvos or smoke Marlboro or buy Tetley teabags or wander around with a Walkman or ...

Novelists nowadays use brands to reveal their characters' personalities. They know readers recognise people by their predilections for Armani suits or Heinz Baked Beans, for Raybans or for Findus Lean Cuisine.

Bruno Mouran and Pascal Rostain, two California *paparazzi* photographers have won themselves tawdry fame and fortune by ransacking filmstars' garbage and publicising the brands they use. It transpires that Liz Taylor drinks Evian while Jack Nicholson prefers Pellegrino, Veuve Clicquot and Becks; Madonna apparently jogs in Reeboks, Michael Jackson washes with Tide and Warren Beatty uses Kodachrome and likes to munch Snickers – to mention but a few of Mouran and Rostain's findings. These revelations would have no point at all if the world were not fascinated by which famous people use which famous brands: but the world is.

Most of us even like to share experiences with people who choose the same brand as we do, recognising them to be folk of a like mind – and obviously rather sensible about their choices.

(I once attended a suave and scintillatingly sophisticated dinner party at which a novelist and a company chairman bickered endlessly over the relative merits and demerits of Fairy versus own-brand washing-up liquids; and they both instinctively knew that their scrap over brand preferences was symptomatic of a deeper antipathy to one another.)[8]

Moreover we are surprised, even astonished, when we discover people using brands which do not gel with our preconceptions: it conflicts with their perceived personality, so it jars and throws us into confusion.

All of which bears witness to the potency of brands in today's world, and to their grip on our perceptions and imaginations.

Simultaneously it bears witness to the ever finer nuances of market segmentation which brands now exemplify.

Even the different washing powder and detergent brands – than which few different brands are less different – are used by dissimilar groups of people. Dissimilar, that is, in what they want from their washing powders and detergents.

We can picture, in our mind's eye, the users of most brands because most brands are used most often by small bands of people. And that is why we can describe the types of people who use different brands with almost amazing accuracy, when asked to do so by market researchers.

If brands were universal they would have no character.

If occasional, so-called 'repertoire' purchasers were of great significance brands would have no character.

So smart targeting involves finding out as much as is humanly possible about existing customers, preferably existing heavy users, and making sure the advertising is right for *them*.

It will then, as we shall see, be right for potential customers too.

This is as true of young, rapidly expanding markets

[8] This point about branding is far from brand new. As The Rolling Stones sang in their sixties classic *I Can't Get No Satisfaction*:

'He can't be a man 'cos he don't smoke
The same cigarettes as me'

as of long-established markets, though most marketing folk find that hard to swallow.

The widely-accepted management dictum 'Keep Close to the Customer' does not say 'Keep Close to the Non-Customer', nor even 'Keep Close to the Potential Customer'.

To many advertisers, much of this will sound quite illogical, not to say daft.

If you want to win new customers – and winning new customers is undeniably A Good Thing – how can it make sense to target existing customers?

Surely, logic must dictate, non-users cannot be that similar to users or they would *be* users. By definition non-customers are different from customers.

Indeed they are.

But *prospective* customers are more like existing customers than they are like the mass of the rest of the non-customers.

This can be shown mathematically, quite straightforwardly.

Let us take a major brand, being used regularly by ten per cent of the population. To achieve a ten per cent sales increase it will need to convert another one per cent of the population to regular consumption.

(I realise this is a simplistic picture – but it clarifies the principles.)

Is that additional one per cent more likely to be similar to the ten per cent now buying? Or to the 89 per cent who will continue not to buy?

Attempting to grapple with this problem, market researchers have tried to find ways of winnowing down the 90 per cent, so that the one per cent among them can be identified. But they have been unsuccessful.

The most authoritative study to date of all the known techniques of predicting purchase behaviour, carried out by the lively and iconoclastic Department of Marketing at Massey University, New Zealand, showed that even for entire product categories – let alone individual brands – predicted purchase rates are subject to a wide margin of error: a margin so wide as to make the predictions, in my view, uselessly unreliable for marketing planning.

And being so unreliable they are unremittingly misleading, because they provide advertisers with the views and opinions of people who purport to be prospective purchasers but who in reality will never buy their products.

The reason there are no techniques which can accurately identify prospective brand switchers is that there are no techniques accurate to one per cent or two per cent.

And that, in turn, is probably because few people themselves have any idea whether or not they are likely to change their purchasing behaviour in the future, so when market researchers ask them to make such artificial decisions they are understandably flummoxed.

Even political opinion polling – the most highly developed and constantly authenticated form of market research – does not promise to be accurate to one per cent. (And that's as well, because it rarely is.)

No media or database can possibly identify prospective brand switchers.

But media advertising can provide them with the opportunity to identify themselves, to spot the advertisements addressed them.

To do so the advertising must first find them. And

it must ensure that they find the advertisements. And this is an increasingly complex task.

It is increasingly complex because while target markets grow ever smaller, and more segmented, the number of media available to reach them grows ever larger, and more segmented.

The number of newspapers and freesheets in Britain grew from 550 to over 1,300 in the decade between 1981 and 1990.

The number of consumer magazines leapt from 1,367 to 2,373 in the same period.

While the television and radio channels keep breeding like busy bunnies.

Matching the media to the target market calls for sophisticated computer literacy.

Yet advertising is one of the most computer illiterate of all modern major industries.

Computers are used for routine chores in the media and finance departments, and the major agencies now do a small amount of computer-based econometric analysis.

It won't do.

Mass targeting is as out-of-date as saturation-bombing; smart targeting calls for advertising directed with conscious precision.

Shamefully little use is made of computerised data-processing to correlate, to pinpoint, to segment, to analyse alternative courses of action, and to home-in on the real, tiny, target markets.

The early attempts at cluster and correspondence analyses in the 1970s and 1980s were crass and crude. So advertising people got bored with the whole idea and threw the babies out with the bath water.

It is true that there are no simple psychographic groupings of the entire populace, of the kind which briefly became fashionable a decade or so ago. It is not possible to parcel the population into a few neat psychographic bundles[9].

But the same does not apply to individual brands, where personality-based groupings clearly correlate closely with consumers' behaviour.

That is the logic of market segmentation, and indeed it is the logic of everything this chapter has been saying.

Advertising people adore re-inventing the wheel.

Occasionally this has its benefits. But when it comes to targeting there is already a mass of information available, gathering dust in data banks which hardly anyone ever visits.

In the years to come more will be needed; and agencies will need people with the mindpower to use it.

Because it is as vital to the targeting of creative work as it is to the targeting of media – if not more.

---

[9] 'There is a ready solution to every problem,' said the American humourist H. L. Mencken, 'it's simple, neat and wrong.'

VI
Fame is the trap

The miniscule size of most target markets means that however hard advertisers try to select media which reach them, cost-effectively and with minimum wastage, the great majority of those who see any advertisement are not especially interested in the product or service being advertised.

This has resulted in the content of advertisements being greatly influenced by audiences who are – in advertising terms – utterly irrelevant.

Inevitably the views of the non-purchasers, who are multitudinous, swamp those of the purchasers, who are few.

This is true of all media, but it is especially true of television.

Television being so compelling and intrusive a medium, viewers can hardly escape seeing the commercials that hit them between the eyes while they are watching.

Print advertisements work differently: readers can self-select the advertisements they want to look at.

A large print advertisement, which gets in the way of the editorial matter, will obviously intrude itself – as it is intended to – but if it is of no interest the reader can, and will, skip over it in an instant.

A 30-second commercial is there for 30 seconds: it cannot be foreshortened.

(If it really enrages you, you can immediately switch channels; but research suggests that few people do so.)

Nowadays the average British viewer watches about 1.5 hours of commercials every week – the equivalent of a feature film.

As we saw in Chapter II, nobody knows how many

press, posters and other advertisements the average person sees each week; but we all know it's a lot.

Regrettably, this endless blitzkrieg of advertisements for products in which, individually, most people have no interest, has led to three dire consequences for the advertising industry.

First, a hopeless over-reliance on awareness as a measure of advertising effectiveness. Second, an unremitting pressure to make advertisements, particularly television commercials, entertaining. Third, the obfuscation of sales messages.

Ever since 1961 when Russell H. Colley published his seminal work *Defining Advertising Goals for Measured Advertising Results,* for the American Association of National Advertisers, awareness has been widely accepted as one of the best available ways to evaluate the success or failure of advertising campaigns.

Colley's thesis was deliciously simple and seemingly irrefutable.

Because so many factors influence sales, he argued, it is rarely possible to correlate sales and advertising.

It is therefore vital to narrow the definition of exactly what any advertising campaign is intended to achieve. Then, as he says:

'Advertising results *can* be measured *IF* specific objectives are first defined.'

In 1961 this was a major step forward. It is still a useful corrective when people with little or no knowledge of advertising demand to be told the causal relationship between advertising and sales. (Except in the simplest of school experiments, causal relationships are always difficult to establish; it isn't just an advertising problem.)

But what kind of advertising results can be defined which can also be measured? Not a lot.

Coupon or telephone response, if they are relevant. Attitude changes, sometimes. Sales, directly, occasionally. Awareness almost always. And that's it.

Unfortunately, to quote Paul Feldwick and Chris Baker:

"There is an insidious 'logic' that can creep into any area of evaluation. This 'logic' runs as follows: first, measure whatever can easily be measured; next, presume that which cannot easily be measured to be unimportant; finally, act as if that which cannot be easily measured does not exist".

Thus has awareness, being comparatively easy to measure, become the universal yardstick of brand advertising.

And it seems logical because building awareness (or fame, as it used to be called) is a task that advertising, almost uniquely, can perform.

And it seems logical because, as Colley showed, awareness is a necessary stepping stone to further action.

And it seems logical because people who do not know a product exists are not terribly likely to buy it; whereas the more people who know a product exists, the more people are likely to buy it.

Knowledge, however, does not necessarily precipitate action. I've known about Guinness almost all my life but never yet drunk any; I've known about IBM for as long as I can remember, but have never yet bought one of their computers; I've known about Playtex bras for several decades now but I rather doubt that I'll ever buy one.

Indeed I can quickly think of another two dozen famous brands, most of them heavily advertised, whose names I have been aware of for years and years, but which I have never yet bought or used, and probably never will:

Abbey National	Dulux	Marlboro	Phyllosan
Avon	El Al	Oil of Ulay	Renault
Brylcreem	Fray Bentos	Old Holborn	Rolex
Butlins	Gucci	Old Spice	Slazenger
Campbells Soup	Levi's	Pampers	Tampax
Clearasil	Lloyds	Pedigree Chum	The Sunday Sport

Note that I have not cheated by taking several brands from a product category. Since I don't smoke, or have a dog, or use men's toiletries, I could have amassed a sizeable list of products of which I am well aware, and which are strongly advertised, but which I shall never buy, from those three product fields alone.

It is not, in most of the cases, that I have made a conscious decision to reject all those brands, it isn't as deliberate as that. But no matter how heavily or how cleverly they are advertised, no matter how high their awareness, I will not be persuaded to buy them.

That is why awareness and sales cannot be directly correlated.

So is awareness among non-potential customers utterly worthless?

J Walter Thompson's sagacious ex-Chairman Jeremy Bullmore argues that my awareness of Guinness, Tampax and the rest has value for three reasons.

I may one day change my tastes (or perhaps even my sex), and I will then purchase the brands I know about and so feel I can trust.

I may need to buy a stout or even a packet of tampons for somebody else, and again I will probably choose a brand I know about and so feel I can trust.

My awareness will often have an indirect influence on others – my children or friends perhaps – and I will encourage them to use brands I know about and so feel they can trust.

All of which is incontestable.

(Though I doubt if anything will ever tempt me to buy anything by Gucci.)

Fame indisputably has commercial value, as all the Hollywood moguls – and Mega Multinational Inc, whom you will recall bought Mini Marketing Ltd on page 15 – have always known.

But what is the commercial value of fame among people who do not go to the cinema, or who do not buy Mini Marketing's brands?

In any event brand awareness is not the same thing as advertising awareness. Inevitably they often overlap and understandably they often get confused.

But brand awareness can be built in many ways, whereas advertising awareness can only be built by ... well, advertising.

And although advertising may be excellent value, it still costs a pretty penny. And in today's fast-moving markets advertisers need to get their pennies back pretty quickly.

No advertiser can afford to wait patiently for non-purchasers to decide to become purchasers at some remote date in the future – maybe, possibly. Nor can advertisers hope to live off the occasional recommendations of non-purchasers – maybe, possibly.

Infrequent purchasers are icing on the commercial cake, and thin icing at that.

A thoroughgoing study published in 1986 by Simon Broadbent and S. Colman found 'little or no association between campaigns' short-term sales effectiveness and their ad awareness effectiveness'.

There is a loose, unquantifiable relationship, but that's as far as it goes.

The leading awareness-tracking research company, Millward Brown International, has recently attempted to explain this lack of a correlation between advertising awareness and sales as being due to delayed responses on the part of consumers:

'Advertising will condition encounters with the brand that will typically happen *months or years* after the advertising was seen.'

Phooey.

Any advertiser who has ever put any kind of response mechanism into his advertising – from a freephone number to a write-in cookbook – will know that response is quick and tails off thereafter.

Retailers see it happen every Friday.

This is hardly astonishing: it reflects the way in which people's memories work.

I may not remember all that many faces I saw on the street yesterday, but I'll remember a great deal fewer from six months ago.

Any advertising agency which can convince its clients that sales increases cannot 'typically' be expected for months or years after the advertising has appeared would have no difficulty at all selling ice-cream to Eskimos.

One can hear them making a presentation now:

'These are wonderful ads, Mr Client. Magical. When they appear they will do simply nothing for your sales. Nothing at all. That will be nice, won't it? Then after a few months – well it could be years actually – your sales will suddenly jump up. Dashed clever, eh? It's what we at Hype, Hope and Bamboozlem call a long-term binomic inverse customer response function. It's all to do with this awareness thing, but I wouldn't bother to try and understand it if I were you. The campaign will only cost six million quid or so, at card rates. If you book now, of course. Time is of the essence, what?'

Enough of such tomfoolery.

To justify itself economically advertising needs to find the right people and persuade most of them to take action. Now.

Or at the very least, very soon.

No advertisers wait years for their advertising to take effect. Nor could they, nor should they.

Advertising must work both immediately and residually.

It must generate responses both today and tomorrow.

It is treated as a revenue-cost by accountants and by balance sheets, rather than as an investment, because it *is* a revenue-cost (though it also provides long-term benefits).

It may take years to pay for itself, but it must *start* to pay for itself forthwith if not sooner.

Not that short-term results and long-term benefits are mutually incompatible.

Indeed it is one of the greatest benefits of advertising, as compared to all other means of marketing communication, that it works both quickly and slowly.

Perhaps that explains why the endless debate over whether advertising is a short-term cost or a long-term investment has rumbled on for so many years. It is neither.

It is both.

But unless short-term results are achieved the long-term benefits will never materialise.

Advertising could not possibly work in the future if it did not work in the present.

If you want to reach the distant horizon you must cut through the waves inch-by-inch.

In advertising those who keep their eyes too firmly fixed on the horizon usually sink before they arrive.

And anyway, as we have already seen, the use of media, particularly the use of mass media, will inevitably mean that the advertising reaches lots of non-prospective customers – the ones on the distant horizon.

Because only a minority of the users of any medium will be prospective customers.

So additional awareness will always be generated as a by-product of media advertising.

But it should never be the objective.

All of this will become increasingly true, and increasingly important, as markets grow more segmented and more competitive in the decades to come.

The fact that lots of people know about his advertising may provide the advertiser with a warm glow but it will not provide him with a warmly glowing profit record.

Awareness among the true target market is indeed a boon and a blessing. But aiming for awareness among the rest is not only an expensive irrelevance, it can be damagingly misleading.

Because the way to achieve a high level of widespread awareness is to produce advertising which is memorable in itself. There is a strong likelihood that such advertising will appeal to the wrong people, the majority, the non-purchasers.

There are literally innumerable examples of this happening, but the most notorious was the launch of Strand cigarettes, which occurred just as I started out on what I laughingly call my advertising career.

Research showed Strand leaping to 90 per cent awareness within weeks of its launch. It was and probably still is, one of the most famous campaigns ever.

Everybody noticed the advertisements, and admired them, and enjoyed them, and talked about them, and went down to their tobacconists and bought something else.

The brand would have been a great deal more successful if, instead of saying the wrong things to everybody, it had said the right things to far fewer, to a tightly defined target market.

Nonetheless advertisers and agencies continue to be obsessed with advertising which achieves widespread awareness, and to congratulate themselves fulsomely when it succeeds in doing so.

But even if campaigns which achieve high awareness do not always succeed, isn't the converse true? Surely campaigns which achieve little awareness always fail?

Not so.

If you are targeting a minority it is wasteful, and therefore uneconomic, to achieve high levels of popular awareness.

There is no such thing as a free awareness level.

And there are plenty of case histories in which sales

increased while awareness (appeared to) remain low.

I put 'appeared to' in brackets because awareness among the true target market may well have increased; but none of the established means of measuring awareness would have reflected it.

Awareness is generally measured among the entire adult population, or among all housewives, or at best among users of the relevant product field (ie all detergent users, or shampoo users, or whoever).

It is never measured among prospective customers, the true target market. It cannot be.

So trying to relate sales to awareness is a bit like trying to predict the results of the next General Election by carrying out opinion polls among the bushmen of the Kalahari desert.

Such is the cussedness of life that the polls would occasionally get it right. (For all I know, the bushmen of the Kalahari desert follow British politics zealously.)

But the bushmen's political opinions are only a smidgen less relevant than the awareness of non-purchasers.

(On two occasions I have been fired by clients when campaigns clearly targeted at minorities failed to achieve high general awareness levels. I don't that much mind being fired when I deserve it – and that has happened too – but on both those occasions the advertisers were, quite simply, wrong.)

However it is easy, in the welter of advertisements that surround us, to see why advertisers feel so pleased if people notice their advertising.

Their spouses will mention it. So will their children. So will their friends. We have all come instinctively to believe – and conventional wisdom dictates – that advertising which is universally noticed will be effective, while advertising which isn't will not.

But as the legendary Bill Bernbach, the creative genius who founded Doyle Dane Bernbach, would insist: it is easy to get noticed – the difficult thing is to get noticed by the right people for the right reasons.

And that leads us to the second dire consequence of the volume of advertising to which we are all exposed.

There is continuous pressure to make advertisements, particularly television commercials, enjoyable.

Because people are bombarded with so much advertising for products which are irrelevant to them, they understandably (if indirectly) put pressure on the advertising industry to produce commercials which entertain them.

So there is a clash of interests between advertisers and viewers.

Re-stating the case that has been made above, from a different angle, the next time you are watching television count how many commercials are for brands you buy or are likely to buy in the near future.

Count the number of commercials which will result in you taking any action at all (apart maybe from getting up and going to the loo).

I'll bet a half-eaten Mars Bar to a can of alcohol-free lager that the percentage is in single figures.

To a non-purchaser, product details in a commercial are irrelevant. And boring. We might reasonably expect the opposite to be true for purchasers.

If you do not own a cat (76 per cent of the population do not), if you do not often drink lager (about 80 per cent do not), if you do not intend to buy a microwave this year (95 per cent will not), then you will not be in the least interested in the cat food's ingredients, the lager's taste, or the microwave's bells and whistles.

So the less product detail the advertisements contain, and the more they amuse you, the more acceptable they will be to you.

Moreover you will say so volubly in market research surveys.

In Britain the most commonly used method of testing television commercials – focus group discussions – has exacerbated the problem.

It is all but impossible to recruit a sample of those who are truly in the market for that particular product at that particular time. So the reactions of those members of the public who attend the focus group research sessions reflects whether or not they enjoy the advertisements they are shown.

Moreover, to compound this problem further, the researchers who run the focus groups, hard as they try to be objective, inevitably prefer commercials which entertain them to those which don't. And there is copious, albeit unsurprising, evidence to demonstrate that the researchers unwittingly influence the respondents' reactions.

So the market research methodology that is now used to pre-test 70 per cent to 80 per cent of all British television advertising is biased in favour of entertaining commercials.

Nor is it only market research that influences advertisers and agencies. Their spouses tell them which commercials they enjoy. So do their children. So do their friends. They themselves respond favourably to commercials they find enjoyable. Creative awards go to the commercials the juries find enjoyable.

We have all come instinctively to believe – and conventional wisdom now dictates – that commercials which entertain us will be effective, and those that do not will not.

Recent research evidence certainly indicates that commercials which are likeable are more effective than those which are dislikeable.

But it isn't necessary for commercials to be amusing, entertaining or clever in order to be likeable; just as it isn't necessary for human beings to be amusing, entertaining or clever in order to be likeable.

Indeed far and away the most thorough study carried out into the subject, by Alex Biel's Center for Research and Development in San Francisco, suggests that for most products the most effective commercials are simply believable, convincing and informative. Being amusing, entertaining or clever, *per se*, is relatively unimportant.

That is not to say that clever and amusing commercials never work. On the contrary, it is easy to think of some clever and amusing commercials which have worked exceedingly well. But these are exceptions, and misleading exceptions at that, because they appear to support and confirm what almost everyone in advertising wants to believe.

As a result innumerable commercials nowadays struggle to be humorous, and to achieve awareness, often to the point of absurdity.

And often to the point of obfuscating their sales messages; which helps to explain why so many advertisements are misunderstood. This is the third dire consequence of inadequate and inaccurate targeting.

My first trivial experience of this phenomenon

occurred when my father, who was about as interested in advertising as most folk, which is not a lot, attempted to demonstrate to me that he was paying caring attention to his son's chosen career.

Once again the infamous Strand cigarette campaign was involved.

'I think those new Strand adverts are jolly good,' he said cheerfully one evening, under the apparent impression that paternal approbation – even for advertisements which had nothing whatsoever to do with me – would be supportive and encouraging.

'I like the slogan,' he went on, 'you're never alone on the Strand. Very clever that is. The Strand's a busy street. Too busy for my liking. But the advert's very clever.'

The greybeards among you will recall that the slogan was 'You're never alone *with* a Strand'; it had nothing whatever to do with the Strand being a busy street.

(An almost certainly apocryphal story, making the same point, tells of the teacher who asked her class to use the word 'judicious' in a sentence: 'Now hands that judicious can feel soft as your face', said little Johnny, proudly.)

My father was a non-smoker, so his interest in the Strand campaign was purely academic (and paternal). We may assume little Johnny was not a particularly heavy user of washing-up liquids.

Unfortunately it is not only such tittle-tattle which proves that advertisements are frequently miscomprehended: copious research has confirmed the fact.

In 1980 the American Association of Advertising Agencies commissioned what is still the most comprehensive study into the subject yet carried out. It showed that nearly every single one of 2,700 American respondents managed to misunderstand some part of 60 commercials they were shown, and that the overall level of misunderstanding amounted to 30 per cent of the total.

The findings held true for respondents of all ages, income levels, education levels, and for both sexes.

Moreover the respondents knew they were in a test situation, and so they were much more likely to have been attentive than they would have been under normal viewing conditions.

In other words, the research methodology almost certainly reduced the real level of misunderstanding, the level that occurs every evening in every home in the country.

Analysing these depressing results, the researchers suggested that nowadays too many commercials are too oblique; that advertising is a peripheral, 'low involvement' form of communication – viewers switch on to watch programmes, not commercials; that advertising is a 'one-way' communication system, in which the advertiser talks to the viewer but the viewer is not required to respond – and 'one-way' communications are always subject to more misunderstanding than interactive two-way communications.

All of these explanations doubtless have partial validity, and contribute in some measure to the misunderstandings.

But my own view is that it is hardly astonishing that people pay little or no attention to, and hence misunderstand, commercials for products which have little or no relevance to them.

At the very least, equally copious research has

proved the converse: people pay especial attention to advertisements which are relevant to them, and especial attention to advertisements for brands and products which they regularly buy, or have recently bought.

For example a recent study by Starch Research in the USA for the *Readers' Digest* showed that users of a product category are 22 per cent more likely than non-users to see an advertisement for products in that category, and 50 per cent more likely to read the copy.

That is why the once-famous 'usage pull' method of assessing advertising effectiveness, promulgated by the late Rosser Reeves in his hugely influential best-seller *Reality in Advertising*, is about as useful as an art director without a magic marker.

'Usage pull' argues that if people who know its advertising use a brand, then the advertising is working.

Whereas the reality of advertising is that people who use a brand look out for its advertising. Why? Because they are interested in the brand, because they are conscious of the brand, because they buy the brand, and because they use the advertising to justify to themselves that they have made the right choice.

Any my guess is that those who use the brand are much less likely than others to misunderstand its advertising.

(But the researchers did not analyse the data in that way.)

The irony of all this is that while universal awareness and enjoyment are unimportant, the target market – because it is interested – will spot, understand and interpret correctly oblique, encoded messages which may mean little or nothing to the public at large.

Nor need the messages be verbal, or formulaic, or

coldly rational. For many products (if not most) the information customers seek will be emotional, and may be better conveyed in images than in lingo.

A picture is often worth a thousand, etc.

In other words (or even pictures), precise targeting need not result – indeed should not result – in stale and stodgy communications.

But precise targeting may well mean that your friends and family, creative juries and lay commentators will not appreciate what the advertising is saying.

The moral for all advertisers is: nobody watches your advertisements more assiduously than your customers.

(Except, of course, the Chairman.)

VII
The creative book

Implicit in the last chapter is the suggestion that advertising creativity – as it is generally perceived – is detrimental to the production of effective advertisements. Well, as generally perceived, maybe.

The question is whether advertisements which the advertising industry dubs creative – which are original and often entertaining, and win the gongs and gain the esteem and spark the applause of both creative juries and the public – are more or less sales effective than advertisements which are not.

Many advertisers now suspect, understandably, that agency copywriters and art directors are so obsessed with winning *lions d'or* and *prix d'honneurs* that they do not give a fig whether or not the advertisements achieve their real, commercial objectives.

Some advertisers go so far as to believe that prize-winning campaigns – usually deprecatingly described as displaying 'so-called' creativity – are *ipso facto* ineffective.

And listening to creative people chatter in the Mayfair pubs and gossip in the Soho clubs would confirm such advertisers' worst fears.

Vulgar words like sales and distribution and profits are never to be heard. Glittering words like gold, silver and even bronze are forever on creative lips.

However the flip side of the *medaillions* is that famous, award-winning campaigns have frequently been outstandingly successful generators of sales.

From Bill Bernbach's brilliant 1960s Volkswagen campaign, through Heineken, Hamlet and Benson & Hedges to the everlasting Brooke Bond PG chimps, recent decades have been spattered with advertisements which have both won ribbons and won sales.

Moreover all advertisers – even the churlishly suspicious ones – agree that advertising agencies' unique contribution to their sales effort is creativity: the ability to conjure ideas out of the air and to express them in persuasive words and images.

The ability to create remarkable advertisements is, in David Ogilvy's memorable phrase, 'the liver and lights of the advertising business'.

In Britain, in 1989, *Campaign* magazine correlated winners of the IPA Advertising Effectiveness Awards in the previous nine years with their success in winning creative awards.

The 28 IPA award winners had proved their effectiveness. But only one of them had won a Designers and Art Directors' Gold, the most prestigious creative plum in the UK. Additionally however, eight had picked up lesser creative trophies.

So almost one in three of the IPA Advertising Effectiveness Award winners gained some sort of creative award or other: not a bad correlation. But then two-thirds of the IPA winners won no creative prize at all: perhaps an even better correlation. (And given the number of creative awards now on offer, almost an achievement in itself.)

On the basis of which results, you pays your money and you takes your choice. It's lies, damn lies and statistics time and again.

The difficulties derive from the fact that there are two aspects to creativity – or at least to creativity as defined by advertising folk.

First, originality. Second, aesthetics.

To blur the problem even more, these overlap. Original advertisements sometimes have aesthetic merit simply by virtue of their originality.

But originality and aesthetics are not the same.

Advertisements must strive to be original, because they must strive to be different from other advertisements.

Few notice all those that look alike; many notice those that are different – like faces in a crowd.

Being different is one way of breaking through the selective perception barrier.

Advertisements for excellent products, and advertisements which are relevantly targeted, and advertisements which appear again and again, will all also break through the selective perception barrier. But less cost-effectively than they would do if they were perceptibly original too.

Originality, or remarkability as David Ogilvy put it, is inherent in maximising advertising effectiveness.

But when it comes to aesthetics, things get more complicated.

Aesthetics – style, design, eloquence, appearance, wit – are sometimes relevant, sometimes not.

The advertising industry likes and admires aesthetically attractive advertisements. So do I. So do many of the population. Housewives pin attractive recipe advertisements on their kitchen walls, students pin stylish clothes advertisements on their sliding wardrobe doors – which indubitably adds a few pence worth of extra mileage to the advertising, and makes advertiser and agency alike feel good about their work.

But the cruel fact is that aesthetically attractive advertisements are neither universally correlated nor inversely correlated with sales effectiveness.

Advertisements are like fishermen's bait.

More particularly, like fishermen's flies.

(Sorry Professor Key. We admen just can't stop ourselves.)

If he wishes to succeed the fisherman chooses bait that the fish will be attracted to, not bait that he himself will be attracted to.

And he uses different types of fly for different types of fish.

His own tastes are immaterial.

Except that some flies are quite exquisitely lovely. Their colours shimmer, they glitter and gleam. And any fisherman with any visual sensitivity prefers flies which appeal to his aesthetic sensibilities to flies which do not.

Interestingly, even much of the language is the same. Famous fly tiers are often described as 'highly creative'.

There is no way to make worms, or groundbait, or most advertisements, sparklingly attractive.

And any attempt to do so would (and occasionally does) destroy their purpose.

But some flies are both beautiful and effective. And everyone agrees these are best of all.

However nobody thinks that the fish, in responding to them, are displaying their aesthetic good taste.

Whereas in advertising the situation is rather more complicated.

Because for some products attractive aesthetics are an important ingredient in the mix: this is obviously true for fashionwear, for furnishings (especially electronic equipment), for perfumes, and for cars; it is also true, if a little less so, for alcoholic drinks, for cigarettes, for many foods and for toiletries; and it appears to be irrelevant for domestic cleansers, and confectionery, for some retailers and for most popular media.

(If you believe *The Sun* and *Woman's Own* are things of beauty and joys forever you have a curious sense of aesthetics. But they are wonderful products.)

Exactly why attractive aesthetics are more important in some product categories than in others is worthy of a PhD thesis in its own right.

All we need note here is that when attractive aesthetics are very important in the product they will likewise be important in the advertising; and when they are not they probably won't.

That is why certain product categories scoop most of the creative awards while others never do.

(When did you last see a household cleanser commercial grab an advertising Oscar?)

Awards juries, predictably, prefer advertisements that are aesthetically attractive.

And as always the aesthetics of the practitioners are likely to be more refined, more subtle than the aesthetics of the customers – because the practitioners are absorbed in advertising continually, day-after-day, whereas the public is not.

Moreover the practitioners – particularly the art directors and copywriters – are good at their jobs specifically because they are more sensitive to colours, shapes and words than most other folk.

So it is less than surprising that the practitioners occasionally get seduced by advertisements which attract them intensely but mean nothing to the public at large.

It is equivalent to the fisherman using a fly because he likes it, forgetting the predilections of the fish. Doubtless that, too, happens from time to time.

There is one other way in which fly fishing is like advertising.

Because we identify with the fisherman rather than the fish, we are prone to think of the process from the fisherman's point of view.

But the fish responds to the fly for its own selfish reasons: it perceives a consumer benefit.

Fishing, like advertising, is a two-way process.

The fisherman and the advertiser cast their lures, in the places they are most likely to be seen, for *their* own benefit; the fish and the consumers see the lure and respond for *their* own benefit. But there the analogy ends.

Fish get hooked, for good and all. If consumers get hooked and don't like it, they have many means of redress.

VIII
A determined tug on the tiller

It naturally seems to me that the argument has so far been straightforward, almost to the point of ludicrous banality, and hardly contentious.

In summary, it goes like this.

Although they are incessantly and increasingly bombarded by a veritable welter of advertisements people respond to only a miniscule number of them.

(For fun I suggested four per cent – but in reality the figure is obviously far smaller.)

People filter out the rest by way of selective perception, which simultaneously shuts out those advertisements which do not interest them and focuses their attention on those which do.

Advertisers can either use people's selective perception to their advantage (classifieds, patent medicines) or they need to pierce it by making their messages intrusive.

For those who may be interested in the product being drawn to their attention, the intrusion will be welcome; for everyone else it risks being a minor irritation.

In any event, and however hard advertisers try, people will still not respond to all that many advertisements because they do not buy all that many branded products and services: a handful of the immense variety now available.

Just as people buy comparatively few brands, brands are nowadays bought by comparatively few people: even the most major brands are bought by minorities.

And significant sales increases can be garnered from even tinier minorities.

So the task of advertising, for the foreseeable future,

will be to discover these minorities, hidden away among the populace at large, and say exactly the right things to them.

This will not be as difficult as it sounds because they will either be existing customers, or be very like them.

However, the process is clouded by the fact that market research, despite its immense sophistication, is still not much good at identifying the wants and whims of small percentages of the population.

It is further clouded by the fact that everybody innately believes famous advertising must be effective advertising, whereas no such correlation exists.

And it has been, and will unhappily continue to be, still further clouded because people prefer advertisements for products which they have no intention of buying – and which intrude upon them – to be enjoyable and attractive.

And they express their predilections both via market research and in personal comments to advertisers and their agencies.

Lacking any more refined means of evaluating their advertising, advertisers have increasingly come to rely on such personal comments, as well as on crude awareness measurements and attitude shifts.

But those measurements are almost never taken among real target markets; and among non-target markets they can be positively misleading, as it is easier to achieve awareness by omitting product details which are boring to non-purchasers (but usually of great interest to purchasers).

And the situation is finally clouded by the entanglement of advertising with aesthetics.

In some product fields this entanglement is a bonus,

in others a danger; but in any event it is unavoidable.

✳   ✳   ✳

All of which makes it sound as though the advertising industry must be in desperate straits. And patently it isn't.

So three closing questions remain.

How come advertising continues to survive, though not quite to thrive, if so much is being done wrong?

What can be done to improve things?

Might there be new and altogether better ways than advertising to achieve the same aims?

Advertising people – who prefer things to be black or white – like to say that this campaign has failed, that one succeeded.

At the Hype, Hope and Bamboozlem agency, where they have rather a neat way with words, they nimbly divide advertisements into two groups: 'All our ads are great,' they say succinctly, 'all yours are crap.'

Advertisers too, if a little less pungently, will say that advertisement A was effective, advertisement B was not.

But the truth is that advertising is a spectral business, best analysed not in blacks and whites but in shades of grey.

Almost all advertising achieves something; the eternal question is, how much?

Consider this simple example.

You've grown a surfeit of apples in your garden and you take some advertisements to sell them.

You may get one customer, or two, or half-a-dozen, or dozens.

If you receive no response at all, the advertisements will have failed; but in the marketplace that eventuality is rare.

Most commonly, the response will vary from dreadful to excellent.

If you wish, and as Russell Colley advises, you can set yourself a goal, a self-imposed target by which you can judge the advertisements' performance.

Obviously you will want to sell sufficient apples to cover the campaign's cost and maybe make a respectable profit.

So that could be your goal.

Or you could ask everyone you know whether or not they have seen your advertisements and if, say, 50 per cent have done so you will reckon your little campaign has done its job.

So that could be your goal.

Setting a goal, however, will not affect the advertisements' performance.

Setting goals reinforces the black/white view of advertising effectiveness.

Goals suggest some campaigns succeed, outright, while others fail, outright. That is not the case.

Setting goals is a desirable management discipline. It is not a reflection of the way advertising works.

It is like saying all males over 6 feet are tall, all males under 6 feet are short.

But men come in an infinite number of varied heights.

And advertising campaigns achieve an infinite variation in levels of effectiveness.

It is my contention that lately the effectiveness of advertising has fallen a few notches, simply because the industry has failed to perceive the consequences of recent developments in the marketplace.

So advertising has grown a little less cost-effective. And this is a matter of much more than minor importance, in view of its influence on consumer demand, and thus on the economic wellbeing of the entire community.

But advertising has not suddenly become impotent. It still works.

Which brings us to the second question: how can it be made to work better?

Easy-peasy.

In three words: focus, focus, focus.

Or if you are one of those people who prefer longer words: target, target, target.

Identify your customers, find out everything you possibly can about them and then lots more.

Forget phrases like mass marketing and mass advertising: focus on the target market and ignore everyone else's extraneous attitudes and views.

Do not be seduced by irrelevant praise or be downcast by irrelevant criticism. Don't be misled by the awareness and attitudes of non-purchasers. Only the customers' views matter, nobody else's.

Finally, if it is true that affluent economies comprise a swarm of minority markets, is the demise of advertising in 'mass' media on the horizon?

Do all the arguments in favour of focus and targeting favour sharper, less wasteful forms of communication?

Direct mail perhaps? Pinpoint door-to-door distribution? Telemarketing? Inter-active video marketing? Catalogue selling? Some means of electronic communication as yet undreamed of?

None of them will replace advertising, at least for

decades to come.

And especially if advertising now gets its act together.

Advertising provides incomparably greater glamour and publicity than other, more private means of communication.

It is nice to get letters and 'phone calls from friends, but far more exciting to see them on television, in a magazine – or even in the local newspaper, provided they aren't there as a result of some heinous peccadillo.

As we saw earlier, media advertising is still an exceedingly economical form of mass communication: it is infinitely less expensive than most of its competitors.

It is easily the most cost-effective means of reaching millions and millions of unknown people, some of whom are, or may become, customers.

For the great majority of products and services, there is no cheaper or more efficient way to track them down.

And increasing efficiencies in the production and dissemination of media should reduce the real cost of advertising still further in the future.

Every couple of years in Britain the Institute of Practitioners in Advertising publishes a cornucopia of case histories – the IPA Advertising Effectiveness Awards – which prove conclusively (in so far as anything can be proved conclusively in commercial life) that advertising pays, when properly used.

In the United States, recent studies reported by Alex Biel of The Center for Research and Development, many of them using high-tech split-cable and bar-code sales measurement techniques, all reach the same conclusions.

Advertising can make a measurable, significant contribution to profitability in the year in which it appears;

and it will usually provide a carryover effect – albeit a dwindling one, unless further advertising is run – in the two years thereafter.

In other words it works both quickly and slowly.

Advertising has survived since Aesclyptoe's days. It will be around for a good while yet.

But having sailed into squally seas it is now drifting dangerously off course.

A determined tug on the tiller is needed.

Acknowledgements

I am indebted to Gray Jolliffe and Andy Tilley, who helped me greatly, albeit unknowingly, with Chapters II and V respectively. I am also indebted to Jeremy Bullmore, who made me think much harder than is my wont.

Finally, I am grateful to Tim Ambler, Pat Kavanagh, Lucasta Miller, Tim Miller, David Morgan, Mark Ramage, Paul Slaymaker and Jeremy Tunstall – all of whom made generally encouraging and invariably helpful comments on the first draft.

Any bloomers, in the time-honoured phrase, are my own.

Select Bibliography and References

J. M. Agostini & M. Brulé, 'Marketing Communication & Consumer Involvement', ESOMAR Seminar Paper, April 1991.

A. Baddeley, *Human Memory*, Lawrence Erlbaum Associates, London 1990.

A. F. Biel, 'Strong Brands, High Spend', *Admap*, November 1990.

A. F. Biel, 'Love the Ad. Buy the Product?', *Admap*, September 1990.

D. Bloom, 'Do We Need To Worry About Long-Term Effects?', *Admap*, October 1989.

BMRB *TGI Summary Report 1991*.

G. Brown, *How Advertising Affects the Sales of Packaged Goods Brands*, Millward Brown Plc, 1991.

S. Broadbent, C. Channon & P. Feldwick, *Advertising Works, Vols 1-6, IPA Advertising Effectiveness Awards 1980-1990*.

S. Broadbent & S. Colman, 'Advertising Effectiveness Across Brands', *Journal of the Market Research Society*, Vol 28 No 1, January 1986.

J. Bullmore, *Behind the Scenes in Advertising*, NTC Publications Ltd, Oxfordshire 1991.

P. Charman, 'Hard Sell Honours v. Creative Kudos', *Campaign*, 19th May 1989.

R. H. Colley, *Defining Advertising Goals for Measured Advertising Results,* Association of National Advertisers Inc., New York, 1961.

K. Crosier, 'Towards a Praxiology of Advertising', *International Journal of Advertising,* May 1983.

D. Day *et al,* 'Predicting Purchase Behaviour', *Marketing Bulletin,* Massey University, New Zealand, May 1991.

A. S. C. Ehrenberg, *Repeat Buying,* (2nd Edition), Charles Griffin & Co. Ltd., London 1988.

A. S. C. Ehrenberg, 'New Brands and the Existing Market', *Journal of the Market Research Society,* Vol 33 No 4, October 1991.

M. W. Eysenk & M. T. Keane, *Cognitive Psychology,* Lawrence Erlbaum Associates, London 1990.

P. Feldwick & C. Baker, *The Longer & Broader Effects of Advertising,* Institute of Practitioners in Advertising, 1990.

J. Gunther, *Taken at the Flood,* Popular Library, N.Y. (1961).

J. Jacoby *et al, Miscomprehension of Televised Communications,* American Association of Advertising Agencies, N.Y. 1987.

J. Jacoby *et al, The Comprehension & Miscomprehension of Print Communications,* Advertising Educational Foundation Inc., N.Y. 1987.

J. P. Jones, 'Over - Promise & Under Delivery', ESOMAR Seminar Paper, April 1991.

T. Joyce, *What Do We Know About How Advertising Works?*, J Walter Thompson, London 1967.

T. Joyce, 'Models of the Advertising Process', ESOMAR Seminar Paper, April 1991.

R. P. Kelvin, *Advertising & Human Memory*, Business Publications Ltd, London 1962.

W. B. Key, *Subliminal Seduction*, Signet N.Y., 1974.

S. King, 'Brand Building & Market Research', Market Research Society Seminar Paper, 1990.

H. Krugman, 'The Impact of TV Advertising: Learning Without Involvement', *Public Opinion Quarterly*, Vol 29 No 3, 1965.

M. Lander *et al*, 'What Happened to Advertising?' *Business Week*, September 1991.

P. Martineau, *Motivation in Advertising*, McGraw-Hill Book Company, N.Y. 1957.

M. Mayer, *Madison Avenue USA*, Penguin, London 1960.

M. Mayer, *What Happened to Madison Avenue?*, Little Brown & Company, Boston, 1991.

T. R. Nevett, *Advertising in Britain: A History*, William Heinemann, London 1982.

D. Ogilvy, *Confessions of an Advertising Man*, Atheneum, N.Y. 1962.

V. Packard, *The Hidden Persuaders*, Penguin, London 1960.

Readers Digest, 'The Disloyal Husband', *Pegasus News*, August 1991.

Readers Digest, 'Go for Product Users', *Pegasus News*, October 1991.

R. Reeves, *Reality in Advertising*, Alfred Knopf, N.Y. 1961.

W. Sykes, 'Validity & Reliability in Qualitative Market Research', *Journal of the Market Research Society*, Vol 32 No 3, July 1990.

J. Walter Thompson, *Lifestyle Trends in the United Kingdom*, JWT London, 1990.

A. Wicks, 'Advertising Research - An Eclectic View from the UK', *Journal of the Market Research Society*, Vol 31 No 4, October 1989.

J. W. Young, *How to Become an Advertising Man*, Advertising Publications Inc., N.Y., 1963.

Index

Response 41, 66, 67, 75, 85, 88
Revenue-cost 67
Rolex 64
The Rolling Stones 54
Rostain, Pascal 54

Sainsbury 44, 51, 53
Sandwich-board 21
Selective perception 22, 24, 29, 42, 81, 85
Sex 38, 39, 51
Skywriter, 21
Slazenger 64
Snickers 54
Sponsorship 14
Starch Research 76
Strand cigarettes 69, 74
Subliminal Seduction 38
The Sun 83
The Sunday Sport 64
Supermarket 14, 35, 50

Tampax 64
Target Group Index 49, 51
Target market 33, 47, 58, 61, 68, 69, 76, 86, 89
Targeting 12, 35, 40, 47, 51, 53, 55, 59, 69, 73, 77, 81
Taylor, Liz 54
Ted Bates agency 43
Telemarketing 14, 89
Telephone response 63
Television 9, 17, 26, 35, 41, 42, 43, 53, 58, 61, 71, 90
Tesco 45, 51
Tetley 54
Tide 54
The Times 30

Toiletries 82
Tracking studies 10

Unique Selling Proposition 9, 39, 43
United States 14, 90
Usage pull 76

Valentine 25, 26, 40
Veuve Clicquot 54
Video Storyboard Tests 23
Volkswagen 79
Volvo 53

Warwick 31, 32, 33, 34
Washing powder 55
Whiskas 49
Woman's Own 83